My Dad is a Lock Keeper

Written by Gemma Bagnall
Illustrated by Marina Pérez Luque

Contents

What Are Canals For?

My dad is a lock keeper. He helps to look after canals so boats can travel along them.

Canals were first made for transport in the 1700s.

Now people mainly travel along them in boats for holidays.

Narrow Boats

Narrow boats are often brightly painted and have interesting names.

Some people live on narrow boats.

They get power from solar panels.
A log-burning stove gives them heat
and they keep water in a big tank.

Canal Locks

Canal water stays flat, so locks help boats travel between low and high water levels.

1. The gates open.

2. The boat enters the lock.

3. The gates close.

4. The lock fills with water.

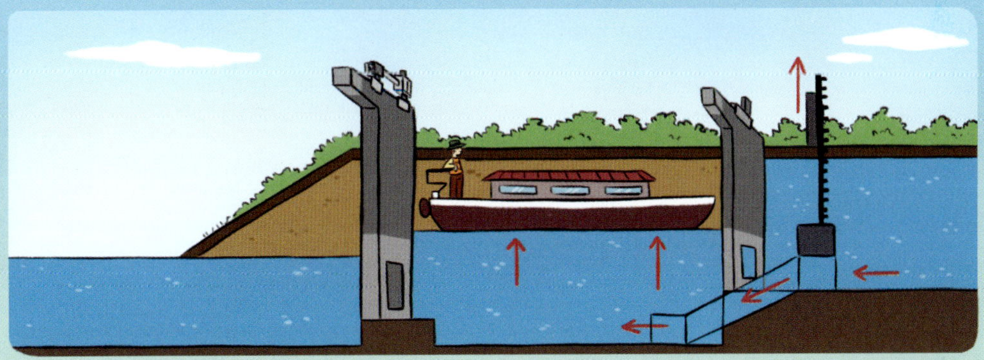

5. The boat exits the lock.

River Locks

River locks are much bigger than canal locks. They can be seen where rivers run steeply downhill.

The water is faster and deeper than in a canal, so only lock keepers like Dad can operate river locks.

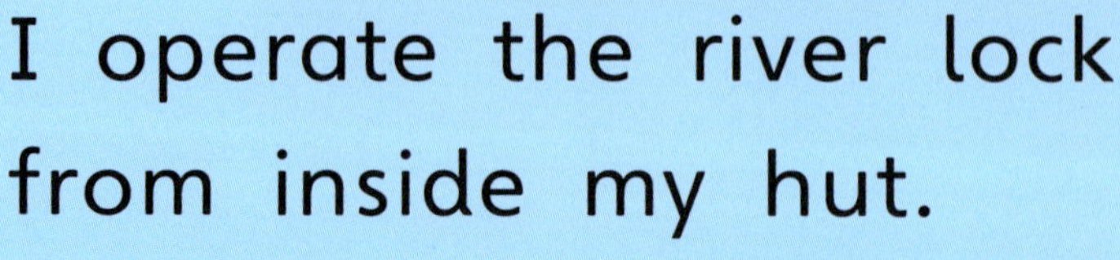

I operate the river lock
from inside my hut.

Buttons let me operate the gates
and make the water level in the
lock go up or down.

Wildlife

There is so much wildlife to spot near canals and rivers.

12

We have
seen otters,
kingfishers,
cormorants
and herons.

Canals Across the Globe

The Grand Canal in Italy is as wide as seven buses!

In Amsterdam in the Netherlands, lots of people travel by bike or boat.

The Panama Canal is a short-cut for big ships. They can sail right through where the land would be!

Index